SPUNKIFY YOUR LIFE

8 SECRETS TO LIVING WITH MORE FOCUS, FASCINATION, AND FUN

Cynthia Mendenhall

Dedication

To all those who have believed in me
and supported my crazy dreams.
You are the best!

Spunkify Your Life
Contents

Foreword

My most favorite thing to do in life is to talk to people and teach them how to walk in their destiny and to live out what and who they were created to be.

In this amazing book, my friend Cynthia Mendenhall walks you through the steps of how to approach living your life proactively with hope and passion for a greater future. For you to live the life that you were created to have, but a life where you just need a little coaching, pushing, and fun to get you moving in the right direction.

In each chapter, Cynthia reveals a secret to living with more focus, fascination, and fun. She

breaks it down into a simple plan and tells you how
to make some simple yet powerful decisions that will change your life. This highly creative and captivating book will renew your insight and refresh your focus.

She has made major life decisions to simplify her life in such a way that her life has become forever better. For years, she has studied and pursued life in such a way that she refuses to settle on leaving life to chance. She purposefully looks to improve her life by seeking to learn from others and then utilizing her knowledge to make personal changes. And not only that, once she grasps those life principles, she does all that she can do through her life coaching, speaking, seminars, and workshops to impart them to all those around her.

There are people in this world who do a lot of talking the talk, but let me tell you, this lady does a lot of walking the walk. She does it in such a way that it brings *spunk* and light into every room, corner, and crevice she enters.

Cynthia has personally inspired me to dream more and not only while sleeping, but she inspires me to bring my dreams into real life by putting those dreams into action by "waking them up."

Live, love life, and overflow with confident hope (Romans 15:13) as you read and discover the secrets to "Spunkify Your Life."

Kim NeSmith
Co-Founder and Co-Pastor
Barefoot Church
North Myrtle Beach, SC

SPUNKIFY

to fill with spunk

— — —

SPUNK

courageous determination

Introduction

Let's go shopping! We can head over to my favorite discount department store, *Ross, Dress for Less*. They carry quality garments, and some high-end name brands, all priced for a small budget. And they allow you to take eight items into the fitting room. Eight!

You've complained about your current wardrobe long enough. Your body has changed lately, your life has made a huge shift, or you suddenly hate everything in your closet.

You'd like to add some items that sparkle or will sparkle you up a little. Your life needs some pizzazz.

For whatever reason—perhaps you like how I dress or trust my opinion—you've chosen me to be your guide.

We flip through hundreds of options and gradually collect eight hangers full of what I believe are great choices to add a little more thrill to your days.

Now for the hard work of undressing in unkind lighting with too many honest mirrors looking on. Vulnerability takes guts.

Dress number one is loose all over, the yellow skirt is too tight at the knees, and the flowy Michael Kors blouse, you claim, will not work with anything else in your closet. Too long, too short, too weird in the arms eliminates the others.

You are happy, and a little relieved, to emerge with two perfect pieces. Once you start wearing them regularly, you love them more and cannot wear them enough. In time, you add earrings to match the top and a perfect bangle and some colorful flats to match the dress.

These new clothes change your overall attitude. Every time you wear them you are excited and like what you see in the mirror. Others notice you are more confident and happy; they inquire. They note the changes you feel. And you are surprised how much difference these small changes have made.

Here's the deal though.

I hate shopping. And honestly, my wardrobe options are a little tired and lackluster. People rarely compliment my clothing choices, and that's okay. However, they often marvel over my attitude and spirit. And they do notice the way I approach life with so much anticipation, enthusiasm, and hope. They comment on my undying sense of adventure and curiosity. They inquire of my unquenchable thirst for knowledge and the learning opportunities it provides.

I once lived days I didn't enjoy, feeling empty and lost. I blamed others, my past choices, and the circumstances that surrounded my life. But after I became single again and my daughters moved away to college, I realized if I was not happy, then it was entirely my fault.

If I wanted a better and more fulfilling future, it was completely up to me to make that happen—not that I had any idea where to start. Just as I am suggesting to you, I started trying on other options. Lots of other options, like multiple trips to many fitting rooms.

The best and most profitable truths I discovered and used to create my wonderful life are the same ones I've gently shared with my coaching clients, friends, and family members over the past several years. Those individuals, in turn, selected a few that fit them best and soon found themselves moving toward a more incredible life full of focus, fascination, and fun.

If you are not thrilled with the style of life you currently are living, it is up to you to change it. You can launder the same old practices week after week, but I'm offering you a few new varieties to try. And I'll stay near in case you want to model.

Keep an open mind as you read each strategy, then at least try every one of them on. We all know things look different on the rack. Feel free to keep the ones that fit you best. Wear them often and accessorize.

It's okay that not all eight will work for you right now. After all, that's pretty typical, right? But as you make small adjustments in your life, the others will be hanging here waiting for a second try.

As your life continues to change and grow, you may find the strange fitting dress of chapter 6 may now fit perfectly. Or that foreign-looking blouse hanging in chapter 4 eventually looks like something the wardrobe of your life needs.

So instead of bargains hanging at the local *Ross*, I offer you a chance at a huge makeover—a complete redesign of the closet of your life—all gathered around the belief that you can make the rest of your life the best life possible.

The thoughts in this little book represent my personal philosophy on life.

Welcome to my closet!

May you accept these suggestions with the same spirit in which they are offered, my friend. And may all your try-on-room experiences be positive and bring goodness, light, and life.

Blessings,

Cynthia

—1—

Feathers in Your Teeth

My oldest brother visited me at the beach recently and rented a golf cart. I had never driven a golf cart before and never explored my neighborhood with one. I giggled, laughed out loud, squealed, and cheered.

After a couple of hours, or six, my voice was hoarse, my hair topsy-turvy, and my eyes brighter than they had been through the entire winter. That night, though, I had to take two ibuprofens because my jaws hurt too much to sleep!

The Joy-Makers™ of life are different for everyone. What makes you smile could be other people, perhaps your children, grandchildren, or best friends.

Others may find fresh flowers, a bubble bath, that first sip of morning coffee, a fuzzy blanket at night, or a steal of a deal on the clearance rack takes them to a happy place—a place that can make their jaws hurt from smiling so much.

Hard to believe, but there are people who cannot readily identify three or five things that make them smile. One lady I worked with needed an entire week to come up with one idea.

Why is this so challenging?

Wives, mothers, caretakers, and especially those in ministry all tend to be givers. We freely give of our time and knowledge. We share our energy and experience. We will even sacrifice our sleep, and our own personal downtime to help others.

Children, jobs, husbands or significant others, parishioners, clients, neighbors, parents, friends, clubs, projects, etc., will drain us dry. And while we may enjoy some of these things we give in to, or that are demanded of us, how much of your day—week—month—year makes you smile?

What are those visuals, objects, activities that make you so happy that the endorphins in your brain bounce, leap, and splash? Make a list, if necessary, so you can easily and intentionally add them into your schedule.

Happiness cures the everyday blues. Smiling, laughing, or thoroughly enjoying something lowers your stress level and can help adjust a high blood pressure reading. Plus, it just makes you more fun to be around.

We all deserve to enjoy more of our life than we do. We need to smile. I understand that life is hectic and you have responsibilities. Everyone feels short on time. But can you spare fifteen minutes?

I've created a combining technique that exponentially returns even the smallest investment of fun and enjoyment. Smile-Maker Math™ works like this: You identify a few things that bring you joy, then you look for ways to combine them. Simple, right?

Here's my example. I love drinking coffee. I enjoy sitting by a pool or other body of water. My body craves sunshine. And escaping into a great novel is one of my favorite pastimes. Now let's say I have fifteen minutes that I have carved out of my day for pure fun.

Quick, what do I choose?

All of them!

In this scenario, I'll take a cup of fresh coffee to the sunny pool area and read one chapter. Bam!

A dear friend of mine, Victoria, loves to explore new places, enjoys long slow walks, and comes truly alive behind her Canon Rebel. Let her find an hour, or an afternoon, and she is gone, combining all of these with a yummy lunch at some new little bistro.

With Smile-Maker Math™, the results are different than regular math. If you combine or add two fun activities together, you do not have a doubled sum, but rather something that feels more like a final payoff of ten times the power.

The more you pack into your fifteen minutes, the more profitable it becomes for you. Soon you will find yourself trying to manipulate an additional five minutes, or an hour.

Whatever time you have, tailor it to suit your needs best at that moment. Some days, maybe less really will be more and your Joy-Maker™ may be nothing more than sitting without doing anything but breathing, or taking a twenty-minute nap. Do that.

Design your little breaks to bring you the most joy possible for the time available. But consider this warning: smiling can be addictive. Often, the more we smile and enjoy, the more we want that in our life.

If you are going to succumb to one vice that helps you through life, isn't this one perfect? No harmful side effects, it's free and healthy, and legal in all fifty states. Plus, if you can get a good hour of outright laughter with a friend or with your brother on a golf cart, then you are probably going to work abdominal muscles that need a little workout too.

Another really cool consequence is that smiling often becomes contagious. Unless you act real creepy about it, flashing a large smile to someone—even a stranger—tends to make them smile back at you. If we keep smiling, the whole world may finally all at once smile together.

And if you smile all the time, it makes the people around you crazy. They start rolling through your Instagram photos or digging deep to see your status updates on Facebook, trying to discover the scoop. They'll be convinced you're up to something or onto some insider trading secrets.

They may study you from a distance, as if they are undercover happiness cops, waiting to pounce from the shadows and yell, "Gotcha!" And that whole imaginary scenario makes me smile even more.

It's fun to keep people curious by smiling genuinely and frequently. Most will never outright ask you what's up.

Once in a great while, you may run into that one outspoken person who may hint about the canary you've swallowed. For that you may want to keep a feather handy to pull from your teeth.

Or you could simply quote Buddy from one of the greatest Christmas movies of our time, *Elf*, "I just like to smile, smiling's my favorite."

Even in the roughest of times, we still need to experience moments of joy. Unfortunately, we all have experiences when we need to find something to make us laugh, especially when we can't or don't want to. Maybe we are too sad or overwhelmed or tired to feel like smiling.   In these times, make sure you have one guaranteed Joy-Maker™ in storage. A go-to situation, event, person, or object that will always turn your down spirit around. Just in case you need it.

That could be an evening with your grandbabies, a mini-shopping spree, a phone call with your bestie, your favorite movie or book, or a long walk alone.

My go-to is the terribly outdated show, *America's Funniest Home Videos*. It's stupid, mostly staged, and I hate it, but one old episode (which plays every day on some channel at some time) will have me laughing out loud so hard that my eyes do that rolly-up thing and I feel like I'm going to pee my big girl panties. Most importantly, though, it transports me out of my blues or exhaustion to a happy place in minutes, when I need it the most.

Do yourself the biggest of favors. Smile and laugh on a regular basis and soon your life will naturally bubble over with happiness and giggles. Those around you can either join in and smile along or just remain crazy curious.

And may you ever so often need ibuprofens to get to sleep because of the pain in your smiling muscles!

—2—

Storage Units in Faraway Places

A past. We all have one. Some are longer than others and some just feel longer than they've actually been. No matter if our journey has been filled with wealth or poverty, acceptance or rejection, easy times or sadness and continual heartache, our past has made us who we are.

If you have lived and loved at all, then you will have regrets. After all, mistakes happen and bad decisions are made. (Yes, there is a difference.)

I find it almost refreshing when someone admits that their past is colorful. You can tell they are not bragging because of the way their shoulders drop; their eyes fix on some distant scene in their memory. Many people find shame hiding in the shadows of their past life.

But a person who's survived hard times and wild experiences usually has a fascinating story of stamina, rebirth, and hope. Usually.

Of course, we will always be subjected to those who clank their past like heavy logging chains around their necks. They assume a posture of "Woe is me." They shuffle their feet. It's safe to imagine that at any time they will put the back of their hand to their forehead, loudly exhale, then say, "But you don't understand—"

We all have a past. All of us. And that past has helped shape us into the people we are today. To clarify, our past is only half of that equation though. Who I am today has been determined by my past *and* my attitude toward it.

Many people do not realize or accept their past as one of the greatest teachers they will ever experience. We are schooled by our blunders, missteps, and by the way others have treated or mistreated us.

If Ms. Past is the best teacher, then is it safe to say that some people are very slow learners, or perhaps, students who refused to engage in order to learn the lessons presented?

Your past should only be considered as the most excellent opportunity to learn and grow. Learning what to do is as important as learning what not to do and why. Yes, you can learn a lot from bad examples.

Learn from your past.

Then put your past behind you.

This second part is most important, especially if you still deal with your past on a regular basis. You see, after mastering the lessons your past has presented, it really has little more to contribute to the quality of your life.

Put the past away and move on! All the negatives—the betrayals, rejections, injustices, and destructive messages—should shake down into a shoe box. We will tape it closed, slide it under the bed, and leave it there. Out of sight and out of your day-to-day thinking and your nighttime wrestlings.

If you ever open that shoe box again, it will be for the sole and temporary purpose of a refresher course, like a two-minute tutorial. Pick up the applicable lesson that needs reviewed, put everything back in that box, secure the lid snugly, then under the bed again in record time.

So often we place fragile items or special heirloom pieces we collect or inherit into storage. We lovingly reminisce about each item as we bubble wrap or tissue paper them. Into the rubber container with the snap-on lid and into the basement or attic or storage unit they go.

It may be ten or twenty years before that tub is opened again. And sometimes, by the next generation after we've passed.

No doubt, those items were precious to us when we packed them away. We would never have imagined parting with them, but let's face it, they held no necessity or importance in our daily lives or we would have made room for them on the coffee table or a kitchen shelf.

Same goes for our bad memories.

Yes, they are significant and we often want to save or preserve them, but we do not need to take them out of that box every single day in order to enhance our life.

Actually, that would waste too much of our time and energy for the type of contribution such an act would offer to our day.

Pack your past away, and refuse to visit it regularly. If this is a constant battle for you, then take your boxed memories two or three cities away, or store them in a rented unit in a non-neighboring state. Somewhere that prevents you from dwelling on them.

Sift the valuable lessons to take with you but do not think you can play with the mess in that shoe box constantly and still have the time and mental focus and fortitude to make a fabulous life here and now.

So whatever your hurts, regrets, and other issues may be, let them go. (I'll try to resist adding those annoying *Frozen* lyrics here.)

Negative memories hinder your forward and upward progression and affect your mood. Your attempted pity parties will repel people rather than inviting them to share life with you.

So what do you have to lose if you choose to continue wallowing in the past?

Life!

You can trade your future for your past and settle for little more than those haunting, disturbing, sad, and troubling memories. It's your choice.

Cynthia Mendenhall

Good luck with making much of a fun and vibrant future when you continue to season it with all of that muck.

The choice is yours alone.

You probably know people who live in their past, always eager to give you the long version to prove their innocence, reciting the names and sins of everyone who has ever wronged them. They eagerly whine and moan about it all. And chances are, you never really enjoy their company.

Avoid being that person.

A certain lady kept bumping into my path. I could barely say hello without her mentioning she was a domestic violence victim. At first, I questioned her current circumstances with concern for her safety.

After several months of these random connections, I finally suggested she think of herself as a domestic violence survivor, especially since the abuse had happened twenty years earlier.

She had lived so concentrated on her past problems and injuries that she continued to drag them around with her. She had no intention of planning her future without the victim filter.

Let your past go.

Here's a little twist. Sometimes, we need to put away the positive past experiences as well. The awards, accolades, carefree times, compliments, and kindnesses shown could roadblock you from a better future.

I once overheard a conversation at a high school graduation party. An attractive family member asked the graduate, "How does it feel to be finished with the greatest part of your life?"

This family member obviously had never moved their mind and memories beyond their high school popularity and successes, although it appeared they had acquired the illusive American Dream before age 40. By that simple question, they voided the value of their spouse, children, career, and life experiences, and all the stuff they'd worked so hard to accrue.

Avoid being this person as well.

Focus on making the present the best it can be; concentrate on making your future fantastic. It's time to move on in the quickest, most efficient way possible, without allowing a bunch of old and unnecessary baggage to hold you back.

One last thought on the subject. Sometimes our past lingers in our minds because of our inability or failure to forgive. Forgiveness is a decision every person must make whether you feel like forgiving, whether you should have to forgive, and even (maybe especially) when you have been mistreated or harmed in some way.

Forgive anyway.

Forgive completely.

Forgive often.

Freedom from the past can be found in the simple (yet seemingly impossible) act of forgiveness.

And don't forget to forgive yourself too.

Often we give grace freely to everyone but our self. Be kind to you; forgive your bad decisions and mistakes.

The unabridged version of who you are will become far greater and more positive when you lay aside your past.

Do you have some packing to do?

—3—

Camera, GPS, and SPF Needed

Vacation mode invokes different thoughts for everyone. For some, getting away is a time of propping your feet up and doing nothing but resting and relaxing. That's their ideal time away, whether on a sunny beach or camping in the desert. As long as they are without a schedule and a to-do list, all is well.

Others pick a spot full of touristy opportunities where they find racks of attraction books, coupons, and fliers at every store and restaurant. They've Googled the top ten things to do in their destination and read all the Trip Advisor reviews.

Some even go to the extreme of scheduling nearly every vacation hour. Their itineraries include places to visit, things to do, must-sees, and restaurants in order to not miss a thing. These are the tried and true tourists. They often look the part and are ready to roll the moment they pull in or land.

Actually, they are ready to roll before they even arrive! Their eagerness bounces them out of the car or the baggage claim area. That's me.

Over twenty-five years ago, a friend and I visited New Orleans together for a conference. No kids, no husbands, just the two of us and anything and everything we wanted to do. We researched. In pre-Google days that meant we checked out library books and interviewed people who had visited there.

One afternoon, as we explored the French Quarter, we paused to take a photo under the Bourbon Street sign. I still smile when I see that snapshot of two classic tourists. I have a chunky camera around my neck; Joyce is holding a folded map. We have umbrellas under our arms, sunglasses on our heads, and black fanny packs (don't judge—it was the early 90s) around our waists. We are wearing new, nearly matching jackets and comfortable shoes. What a sight!

But that photo reminds me to prepare for anything and to enjoy everything. And that cheesy smile of mine begs me to do that every chance I get, regardless of where I live or visit.

And it has become a way of living, a reminder to approach every single day as a privilege and to live with gratitude, with eyes wide open, ready to explore and enjoy.

And, to always be willing to ditch the itinerary, or my plans, in order to experience an opportunity that presents itself unexpectedly.

What would your life look like if you *lived* like a tourist?

Rather than put on the tourist mentality once or twice a year, what if every day or every week became filled with anticipation as you planned something fun to include into your life?

It's not difficult.

Brainstorm activities that would entertain you most or do some research on your hometown. The Facebook Events tab shows fun things scheduled all around your area, sometimes months in advance. Local newspapers usually tuck away small announcements of current happenings.

Discover a small band to follow, join a social club than meets weekly, or meet up with others who share a common hobby or interest. Make a list of new foods or restaurants to try. Take a walk or bike ride in a different neighborhood than usual. Read a novel in one day, because you can. Sit in the sun. Visit a comedy club, take a long drive, or check out the community theater.

Ask friends and work associates what fun they've found to do lately. Or scroll through everyone's Instagram posts and Facebook status updates for new ideas.

Few people spend the money to go on vacation only to sit in a recliner and watch TV. If you are in that small number, then this type of thinking may never be a good fit for you. And that's okay.

For the rest of us, though, never stop exploring. Think in positive "what ifs" often. "What if I turn right instead of my usual left here?" or "Wonder what they are building over there?" Then go see.

Start a list of places to visit and things to do, then estimate the amount of time it may take to accomplish each. Post this on the fridge or stick it to the back of the TV remote and add to it often.

Sometimes a chunk of time to do something fun opens unexpectedly, but a common problem is having a single idea of what to do or where to go. We end up wasting that free time thinking and researching rather than enjoying it. If we do come up with an idea, more than likely there is not enough time left to execute it.

By having the research already done, with the time requirements estimated, you can easily capitalize on those random moments when you get home from work earlier than expected, or when you awake two hours before your alarm on a Sunday.

The real challenge in trying to implement this style of living is the necessary shift in your attitude. You must remain open to try new things, even if you must do them alone.

I've taken nearly a year's worth of improvisational comedy classes where I learned that the foundational principle of improv is "Yes, and." When performing you never negate, dismiss, or refuse an offer from a fellow improviser.

Let's say I am handed a hamburger on stage. I will accept that hamburger and be excited over it although I have not eaten beef for over twenty years.

The "and" part comes as I add to the offer I've been given, "Yes, this burger looks amazing, and I want to share my sweet potato fries with you."

So my classmates and I have been trained to accept every single offer, and to heighten or build on it, until we have a full-blown scene. Otherwise, the scene pretty much ends before it's begun, especially if I refuse the initial burger offer.

You will only have good scenes—a better story and a fuller life—if you practice saying yes to every offer, whether it's something you like or not.

"Yes, I'd love to go to the zoo with you, and we'll take pictures with the hippos."

I once worked with a single-again woman in her late forties who craved a big, out-there kind of life. But she refused to wiggle or bend her routine in any way. Every Tuesday absolutely had to be laundry night, Thursday was grocery night, and Saturday morning was cleaning time. No exception. Ever.

Which is fine, if that is the life you desire, but this particular client wanted adventure and excitement, or at least she claimed to. She would become a little agitated with me for having so much fun with my friends, but could not fathom that I would leave dirty dishes in the sink and the dryer full of towels in order to do so.

Be careful that you do not get so locked into a self-imposed schedule and iron-clad rules that you negate every opportunity you are given. Even if the laundry must wait until Friday, all will be well and you may just be happier for having chosen to do something new and exciting to try.

This same woman refused to try foods beyond chicken and potatoes in their many forms, mostly those that would suit a 6-year-old. That means she turned down every invitation to Asian, Mexican, Greek, and Italian dining.

Yet, every single year, this lady goes on a weeklong vacation with family where the posted photos show her smiling in all types of adventurous settings, including interesting food choices.

She has simply never learned to live like a tourist in her everyday life and where she resides. And my guess is that she will always remain closed to new experiences, refuse to break her routine, and therefore never enjoy the larger part of her life.

It's a comfortable mindset, and often a comfort zone issue, that holds people in their mundane lives of routine and responsibility. Somewhere along the way they too have bought into the idea that fun is only for Saturday night, or one week a year.

Is there a compelling reason to limit fun and adventure?

Growing up, and especially growing old, does not necessarily equate to pleasure naturally. At least my experience has been that you simply do not grow into a fun person. So you must make that happen. Be intentional about it. Really, it is okay to be careless for an hour when you "should" be working on a project.

That type of irresponsibility will more than likely not topple your empire. No more than doing something unpredictable will threaten your reputation. Laughing uncontrollably in public will not smudge your image.

And, for goodness' sake, grabbing groceries a day or two late does not signal the end of the civilized hierarchy that has evolved in your household.

Plus, sometimes it is just plain fun to live a little—just a little—on the rebellious side of routine and ordinary. Refuse to let the status quo win. Take on the tourist mentality and fully act out on even the smallest adventures every chance you get.

Try it.

I dare you!

Hawaiian-flowered dress and flip-flops, optional.

—4—

Designing Women Win

A familiar quote says, "Life is what happens when you're making other plans." And from what I see, that's more than a quote.

Too many people tend to live without any thought to planning their lives or designing their futures. I call it default living, where they sit back and allow life, or others, or situations, or circumstances to determine their future.

The days, weeks, months tick away and without warning these folks wake up as 50-year-olds without much hope.

Dreams?

Oh yeah, those.

"I put those away when . . ."

Goals?

"Well, I messed that up when I . . ."

And although their future does not feel appealing, they think they are powerless to change it. So they go on with living an uninspired and mundane life as they flip the calendar toward their eventual demise.

For some, the difference between living and dying is basically only the breath in their lungs. Time moves forward, but nothing in them does.

You find them at Walmart or Kroger, shuffling their feet toward the eggs, shoulders slumped, mouth frowned. Everything is a chore. They've forgotten how to enjoy their days and have allowed their Hope Tank™ to run on empty for far too long.

Of course, not all who default their lives are this pitiful or obvious. Some personalities accept their lot and make the most of it, but will their mere acceptance be enough to thrill them out of bed every single morning for the next thirty or forty years?

Probably not.

Is there hope?

Absolutely!

The more proactive approach to a fabulous future puts you in charge of designing the type of one you want.

Designing your future takes a little more time and energy than defaulting it, but the payoff is worth everything you invest and more.

Think of your future as a cross- country sightseeing trip. First, you need to determine your final destination. Then you'll want to make a list of all the things you want to experience along the way. Next, you map out your route to ensure that all of your must-sees are scheduled.

The final draft of your itinerary, we know, will more than likely not dictate the trip to the minute as signs for the world's best homemade ice cream, or the nation's largest jackrabbit statue will be too inviting to ignore.

The same is true for life.

Not to sound too morbid, but our final destination is pretty much decided. Now what would you like to accomplish along the way?

It's a pretty solid fact that if you don't have a plan, then you'll never be on track to accomplish anything you've identified as important. Those desires will remain on a fridge list or in a Someday file on your hard drive, ignored forever.

But your heart won't forget.

Life does need a bit of an itinerary. Most often this looks like a vision or dream board, bucket list, timeline, or goals sheet.

By designing a plan for your life, regardless of what format you use, and posting it where you will see it routinely, you will feel some kind of tug or reminder of your dreams for the future.

And while it's fine to detour when something enticing appears, you'll at least have a solid plan of where to get back on course, rather than wandering in the wilderness for the next forty years, or endlessly chasing rabbit holes of empty promise.

I visited a friend of a friend's home lately and noticed a sticky note posted on the side of the fridge. A child's plastic alphabet letter helped secure its position. The note had a title: "I want . . ." and then listed several bulleted lines in clear and careful handwriting.

The one that caught my attention was "visit Italy." Good talk point, I thought.

Later, as we sat at dinner, I asked across the roasted asparagus, "When are you visiting Italy?"

Confusion, mixed with near-fear, flashed in our hostess's eyes a half-second until I gestured toward her fridge list.

"Oh, that silly thing." She faked a laugh and batted the notion away with her left hand. "Probably never."

"Why not?" I was aware of my prying.

She hesitated as if the list had been created on the fly or by someone else. "It's—it's impossible. Too expensive, too far away, and I wouldn't want to go alone." She looked me in the eye for two seconds then added, "Yeah, that one will never happen." This time her chuckle and swipe at the air felt a little more forced.

I let it go after another two seconds of piercing eye contact. But I thought later: This woman is barely fifty, if that, and only has four or five items she hopes to accomplish in the next thirty to fifty years. Is it possible she is not serious about any of them?

I wish I could remember what followed her Italy wish on the list.

Like many people, this woman saw only impossibilities and excuses; I saw how many ways she could make that happen. She just needed to believe it could, then design her life and take those designs seriously.

How much would the trip cost and how long would it take to save that much? Even if it's ten years, so you go in ten years. But you go to Italy! Too far? Planes go from here to there every day, multiple times. And alone? Consider taking the single-again lady to your left who said, "I've always wanted to see Italy."

Don't get caught up in the impossibilities to the point you dismiss your dreams.

If you've always wanted to go to college, go now. It is not too late. Do you hold a secret desire to write a book, to photograph professionally, to sing publicly, or to take gourmet cooking classes? Do it! Climb a mountain, visit an island, or watch an East Coast sunrise and a West Coast sunset all in the same day? Then go for it!

Decide what you want to do, see, and accomplish before you reach your final destination. Then plan to make those things happen by creating a long-term itinerary and working that plan out step-by-step, with patient determination.

We can create excuses all day long and spend our entire life not fully living any of it. Or, we can plan to make the most of every single day and strategize a future full of the things we most want to experience.

Dream big.

Then collect your thoughts on how to make the impossibles come true.

Design your future now to ensure that your next half will be your best half.

—5—

I Gotta Be Me

In 1949, Glenn Ford said, "We are all three people. The person we think we are, the person the world thinks we are, and the person we really are."

Teenagers seem to be the best at this split person routine. Taylor is a cooperative daughter, a great student, a ferocious volleyball player, and kind to her little brother. That's her parents' version anyway.

But to her friends, who are her world, Taylor is the first to agree to every party, every red Solo cup offered, and every guy who shows the slightest interest.

Cynthia Mendenhall

Taylor describes herself as a good girl who just wants to have a good time.

Just because we grow up does not mean we naturally grow closer to becoming one person, the real, authentic version of our self.

Ever notice when you go to a symposium or special event, how perfectly fixed and delightful all of the attendees are? Every lady looks all pulled together, dressed up, engaged, and smiling. This happens in churches way too often. Like no one here has stress, was running late, has doubts, is in a grumpy mood, or had an argument with their family in the car on the way over?

This practice of putting on different faces and personalities for different situations is a big problem for many, and especially those who wish to please others.

Unfortunately, after years of practice, our chameleoning abilities become quite natural to the point they feel normal to us.

Normal, but exhausting.

You see, at some point, our little circles of people may overlap and we can be left with a huge identity crisis. We've suppressed our words, painted on smiles, and faked happy so many times that we lose track of who we really are at our core.

And talk about a crisis! When thirty-, forty-, or fifty-year-olds still operate in teenage mode, a great deal of fallout occurs for them and for everyone else around them, including children, spouse, parents, and colleagues.

A childhood friend once lamented to me that her mother would be throwing a fit, screaming insults and threats at all four kids. Her eyes bugged out and the veins on her forehead bulged. She sometimes would even have a flyswatter in her hand, chasing and smacking the air and them as her outburst continued.

But as soon as the phone rang, this same irate mother instantly smoothed her skirt and answered in the very sweetest of Sunday morning voices.

It seemed to be a common incident; at least she talked about it often. It confused her little nine-year-old self. Was her mother not really mad? Did she just fake her happy hellos?

Not only does this type of repeated behavior confuse, and perhaps threaten those around you, it also confuses and threatens the truest essence of you! That's probably why so many adults walk around not having a clue who they are.

When we act out according to the way others expect, or because of the way we want others to perceive us, then we put ourselves in a continual state of misalignment. At best, it's uncomfortable and tiring. At worst, we become erratic, unhappy mongers of deceit.

I've always been the cut-up in our loud and fun family. Therefore, it became my implied assignment to bring the party spirit to all of our family functions.

During that same time, though, I was an overwhelmed working mom who battled seasonal depression. As secretly as possible, of course.

I would sit hours in a chair, lethargic and crying for no reason other than I could not stop. That is, until Sunday dinner, or someone's birthday, or Christmas morning. Then I would bully myself into hair, makeup, and the biggest obligatory smile. After all, the party must go on whether I felt like it or not.

But how unfair and unhealthy for me, my family, and mostly my daughters.

The real me—that third person—would scream, "Fraud! Fake!" And that made the whole situation worse.

A lot of times we attempt to keep peace, save face, or be everything to everyone, but in the end, diminish ourselves or crush our own soul to pieces.

We readily sacrifice our true selves—our identity—or rather, we allow it to be stolen from us.

The ancient Greek aphorism, "Know thyself," is a good first step to start the process toward becoming closer to our truest self. Take time to know who you are—who you really are. In private. On good days and challenging ones. Know yourself better than anyone else knows you. Learn what makes you tick and what ticks you off.

You are a beautiful creation and were made like no one else. Your uniqueness is a pleasant gift you can give to the world if you are willing to define and live that out. And, it is the best gift you will ever give yourself.

Put away the person you think you are. Be completely honest with yourself, then start gradually sharing the most authentic version of you to your closest circle, whether they like it or not. Once you identify that version, carve it in stone and share it with everyone you meet.

William Shakespeare wrote, "To thine own self be true," and there could not be better advice for this second step. After discovering who you truly are, then protect that with all you've got.

You can be flexible without compromising. You can give, laugh, and love without reverting back to a split identity.

When I was finally able to align myself, I became happier, more settled, and way more comfortable and confident. I slept better and looked forward to being myself with the people who loved me best and most. [My one big exception is the 5:30 a.m. mean monster I am. Apologies to my fellow exercise ladies who witness this twice every week. I'm not a morning person but I'm working on it!]

At first this authentic type of living may make you feel artificial, and you'll find it challenging to combine or align your divided persona, but with practice, it makes life so much easier and happier. This is important. Trust me.

In order for you to live the spunkiest life possible, you must put away the masks of what others see and want, and the mask of who you are trying to be.

And just be you.

Completely exposed, but the perfectly aligned you.

Only then will you encounter true joy and peace.

—6—

Nothing Bad about a Good Fence

Our lives can only become as good as the things we allow in and the things we don't.

Limits and boundaries are popular terms in time management, business training, and relationship coaching. There is a solid argument that we need to incorporate those practices into our everyday lives.

Robert Frost said, "Good fences make good neighbors," which implies fenceless neighbors could hold challenges.

We need to build some fences if we are going to have any control of our schedule, and ultimately, of our life. Without a few limits we will soon stretch in ten different directions until we start to fray around the edges, or perhaps rip right down the middle.

No matter how strong or strong-willed you are, you cannot live a stressful, maxed-out life without that pace eventually biting you in the butt. It is necessary to take breaks, set parameters, and be kind to yourself if you want to continue making an impact in your little corner of the world.

Setting limits—and sticking to them—at home, at work, at church, and in all of our relationships will feel challenging. More so when we love the people involved or when we try to give for a higher cause.

Not everyone in your life has a bulldozer personality, and not every volunteer opportunity requires 40+ hours per week, but guard against those who tend to push you around or organizations who try to pull too much of you away.

Saying no has never come easily to me. I admire those who simply say it with flair and avoid making an excuse or justification for their no.

How easy is it for you to say no?

An older gentleman from my hometown taught leadership classes to junior high and high school students. One of his points has stuck with me all these years. It went something like this: 'If you say yes to one thing, you've eliminated the opportunity to say yes to a whole lot of other things.

You need to measure out offers, people, others' problems and crises, demands, and opportunities. And you do that like this: Picture a large spaghetti-type strainer as the gatekeeper of your fence. I call it the Feed/Drain Filter™.

To be fed is to feel nourished in some way or a multitude of ways. We're talking physically, mentally, financially, emotion-ally, spiritually, relationally. To be drained is to become depleted in one or several of those same ways.

Using the Feed/Drain Filter™ as the judge, you now simply ask yourself if an event or person will feed you or drain you. Am I going to be nourished or depleted if I say yes to this opportunity?

Spending time with a friend can make you happier, make you a better person, help you think more clearly, give you better perspective, or just make you laugh. (Laughter, by the way, is way too undervalued.) Time with this type of friend is worth whatever it may cost in other areas of your life, like sleep, coffee money, or dessert calories.

If you are refreshed and cheered by someone's presence or by an activity in your day, then leave that in your schedule. You may actually want to include more of those types of people and activities.

On the flip side, though, when someone or something depletes you of energy and time, or becomes more frustration than not, then you must delete those things or people from your life, as much as that is possible.

I recently made a new friend who expected a lot from me: time, enthusiasm, optimism, wisdom, free coaching, dinner meetups, and prayers. In return, she encouraged me with her compliments and kind words. But as her expectations (and eventually, demands) grew, she tipped our relationship way too far on the drain scale. I had to end our friendship in order to save my life.

And by that, I do not mean I was suicidal or that she would have physically harmed me. It's just that if I had continued to try to please her, eventually I would have been living her version of my life rather than the exciting life I was trying to create in line with God's plan and purpose for me.

Do you see how important this can become for you? When you take time to design your life, in line with your divine purpose, you cannot allow others to derail, discourage, or drain you.

Here are a couple of other examples.

Following a favorite author may add so much joy in your life that the time and money spent on a book will pay doubly in intellectual stimulation, emotional tugging, and quiet time. Keep that activity.

A new hobby may thrill you but require so much time and money that it depletes your schedule and bank account. Cut it.

Currently, the part-time job I work monopolizes my time, zaps my energy, but pays my rent. The depletion, in this case, is necessary for the return of shelter and food.

Does this all make sense?

It's not always easy to measure this out in the moment. You may need time to jiggle a certain activity or relationship through the Filter™ retrospectively. But do not allow your life to run on cruise control, going through the motions without question.

Shake that Filter™ on a regular basis as changes are sure to come. As you get closer to reaching your life's purpose, then there will be people, hobbies, events, and places you outgrow along the way. Others, you will need.

Using the Feed/Drain Filter™ will help give you the crucial perspective to set the necessary limits to avoid complete depletion. Using it often will help to assure that you are continually nourished in every area of your life.

Just as successful business leaders do not hang on to people who are no longer of value, retail owners discount tired items to get them out of the door.

Do not be tempted to suck it up and deal with someone because you feel sorry for them. And those miscellaneous things in your life that demand constant attention, feeding, or dusting had better add enough value to make them worth keeping.

Of course, as with everything, there are a few exceptions. We simply cannot and should not turn our backs on aging parents, dependent children, spouse, and God-given assignments, no matter the amount of time, money, and energy they drain from us.

That's not to say the implementation of a couple of limits wouldn't better serve everyone.

When full technology integration first hit classrooms over fifteen years ago, teachers had to justify the value added by its use. We all know that teacher who would show his classes *Ferris Bueller's Day Off* from a DVD player with a ceiling-mounted, remote-controlled projector flashing the scenes onto a $2000 Smartboard. But with all of that, no technology value was added, even if he hooked into the wired stereo system.

Do not get into the mindset that everything and everyone that wants a piece of your life will add value to it. If nothing else, be skeptical that no value will be noticed, then search to prove your theory.

Life is too short to allow others to dictate how you should live. People who establish limits—boundaries or good strong fences—are usually happier and appear more stable and in control.

Determine what you wish your future to contain, then build some fences to make sure it does. And remember, while little white pickets are adorable, sometimes the chain link variety with razor-wired top are necessary.

Feed and nourish? In.

Drain and deplete? Out.

And if you can't determine the value added, then perhaps it's time to admit there is none.

In a depleted state, we have nothing left to offer others or ourselves. When we are fed and full, we can feed and fill others better.

Shake that Filter™ often.

—7—

Order Fancy Invitations

Quick! Tell me three things someone close to you does to interfere with their own happiness.

We all know a friend or colleague who needs to end her relationship, waste less money on jewelry so she can pay her electric bill on time, say no to her child more often, or either stop complaining about being fat or quit eating a Snickers and a bag of Lays after lunch every single day.

Now, list your faults and weaknesses. Not quite as easy, huh?

Typically, perspective flows freely from us to others, yet we cannot give true perspective to ourselves. That's a job better outsourced every time.

This clarity we have with others doesn't only work on their bad decisions or mistakes. We also see others' positives at about 20/20 as well, while inspection of our own good traits seems to limit our visual acuity again.

My friend, Nicole, is kinder than she realizes and more generous than anyone else I know. Her hair is beautiful; try as I might, I cannot see the frizzy mess she sees in the mirror. All three of her kids are respectful, gainfully employed, in monogamous relationships, and living independently in their early twenties. That alone is huge these days, yet she questions her parenting.

Nicole's calm wisdom penetrates my heart whether given by phone or over coffee with a side of bacon. Sadly, she sees none of that either. She is too close to what feels like the crazy in her life to see any objective perspective about it. We all are.

All we need, though, is for someone to speak those truths to us. And point out the things, good and bad, we cannot recognize, no matter how closely we study the situation. I do that for Nicole and others. She and others do that for me.

Consider this. Your eyes were designed to look hundreds of yards ahead of you, yet it is difficult, if not impossible, to clearly see the things within their closest proximity: your nose, lips, cheeks, and eyebrows.

Sometimes life may need a small adjustment to become easier, more fun, or less worrisome, but we cannot make that shift if we do not realize a problem exists. We need someone to tell us or show us the necessary shift we need to make.

Here's a silly, yet poignant, story as an example.

My daughter asked, "Do you have any straws?"

"Yep, cabinet by the fridge."

She opened both cabinet doors and stood staring.

"Middle shelf," I offered.

"I don't see straws."

"Oh, you have to move those three small boxes of tea."

She removed the three boxes of tea, grabbed a straw, then looked at me slightly confused. "You must never use a straw?"

Her puzzled look hit me square on, and in that moment, her perspective—specifically concerning my cabinet configuration—revealed my idiotic practice. You see, nearly every single morning I use a straw to drink my smoothie. And for over a year, I'd been removing three boxes of tea to get one.

Her perspective helped me see something so obvious, yet so obscure.

In a more serious scenario, I sought out Debbie and introduced myself when I was at my lowest. Someone had told me she had about a ten-year head start on messing with the muckings of divorce. I pursued her and gave her permission (or maybe begged her at the time) to help me sort out some perspective that I was too devastated to otherwise find. As she shared her experiences, and weekly sorted through my drama, we cemented the deepest friendship. Nearly ten years later, we are still Perspective Partners™, still speaking truth and direction into one another.

One general problem we often experience is that the people around us could offer a solid perspective on our practices, attitudes, opinions, and bad habits. But they don't.

Chances are if we are related to or live with someone who potentially knows us best, we may not be open to their viewpoint on our life. Usually their insights feel more like criticisms with nothing constructive intended. They probably learned long ago that life is better for them when they keep quiet about your life.

No matter how many good friends you have in your life, most of them will never tell you the truth either.

Perhaps your relationship is too valuable to them that they fear pointing out an annoying quirk may push you away. They simply are not willing to compromise your friendship, so they allow you to continue chewing with your mouth open even though everyone in the office is sickened by it.

Other friends may build an invisible hierarchy in your relationship and do not feel qualified to point out a shortcoming on your part. Still others may worship you and be blinded by the way you laugh too loud in public.

Weaker friends may not be confident enough themselves to verbalize an opinion without being asked for one directly. Some people fear saying anything negative ever.

Maybe your friends hold back because they were taught the Thumper Principle (from the movie, *Bambi*), and refuse to say anything if they can't say something nice.

Or, they do not dare cross that biblical line of finding a speck in your eye while hiding a whole log in theirs.

Whatever the reason—and there could be many more—just know that the average person is not going to speak up unless—*unless*—you invite them to do so.

This is vital.

Once you establish a safe zone where friends are asked and expected to speak the truth of their perspective, then you no longer risk going through life not seeing your own nose which is obvious to everyone around you.

So select a few people whom you respect. This does not mean you must find people who have everything together and are living a perfect life. Just identify people you trust and those whose opinion you value.

Then ask them to advise or solve or listen. Once others are given permission, they will most often gladly honor your request and do so in kind and helpful ways, even if they start a bit hesitantly at first.

Asking for perspective does not make you weak or appear uncertain. Seeking guidance, especially in key areas so you can tweak and change, is a significant step in improving your life overall.

A final warning: We all know a person or two who speaks boldly into everyone's lives all the time, whether it's good, necessary, or appropriate. Stay clear of accepting anything this type of person suggests. Sometimes the people who act as the town crier are overdue for a little perspective tune-up of their own.

Otherwise, intentionally seek and build relationships that will act as kind mirrors to you. Encourage those people to speak into your life regularly.

Whether you use an accountability partner, a mentor, a life coach, or a friend does not matter as long as you get the important perspective you need so that you will always keep your straws at the front of the shelf.

And make your life the best life possible!

—8—

The Strength of Your Strand

Whether you have rare and exotic pearls or a ten-dollar strand from Walmart, you have an accessory that is classy and timeless. Add them to a T-shirt or your little black dress and you achieve a pulled-together look, even if your hair is a mess.

We all create our own strand of pearls. Every little experience we allow into our life represents a pearl added to our own custom-made strand. In the same way our necklace can be made up of authentic underwater gems or fake man-made plastic, we can fill our days with valuable people and activities, or cheap imitations. Not that the world may ever know, but you will.

Do you agree that we all want to wear (and create) the absolute highest quality necklace we can?

But here's the even bigger deal. Your strand of pearls will only be as strong and sturdy as the actual cord itself. Although you never see that internal cord, its value is critical.

That inside string is what holds all the pieces together; therefore, the necklace is only as strong as that inner strand.

I once had a long necklace full of natural hematite beads. I've always loved that gunmetal-looking color and enjoyed the metallic feel around my neck. Each bead was small, about the size of a whole peppercorn.

One day as I leaned forward, that necklace caught on a drawer handle. The strand of simple cotton snapped and sent beads bouncing all over the bathroom floor. I gathered them in a zippered sandwich bag where they sat for weeks.

Finally, I bought a 20-pound test fishing line and used that to restring them. I wanted to ensure the one thing that held all the beads together would not snap so easily again.

The same is true for life.

We continually collect little pearls along our journey. They look like conversations, experiences, activities, time with friends, hobbies, and learning experiences. But notice how none of those are connected in a consistent and cohesive way?

Years ago, I felt like the beads of my life just bounced around inside a little plastic bag. I could hold them up to show them off, but how impressive is a plastic bag of disconnectedness?

Finally, I found a cord—the finest and strongest and most reliable of all cords—on which I could strand all my beads of life together side by side, in an organized and interconnected way.

Allowing God to become the inside strand or cord, and inviting him to hold all the pieces of my life, allowed everything to feel a little more together and calm.

And when I used his instructions to care for my great pearls of life, a certain polish and charm was added to all of them. He made them and me classier, if you will.

Every one of us was created by him, made in his own image. The overall intention of our life is to become the greatest version of who we were uniquely designed to become.

To not allow or trust him with stringing the pieces of our life together almost seems like an attempt to live in chaos and frustration. Feeling disjointed and scattered, like the beads of a broken necklace bouncing on the bathroom floor, is a choice we make, whether consciously or not.

Without the strong strand of God running through our life, we will experience little more than constant turmoil and unending struggle. Our days will lack purpose, and our nights become restless or sleepless. Fear will bark at us and doubt will take a bite of our confidence and hope.

Our search for meaning, and for a larger purpose, will never end, as we hold our plastic bag of pearls tightly to our chest.

To thread the pieces of your life together with anything or anyone but God will be a futile practice that could last a lifetime. It's not uncommon for people to try to find their strand in a relationship, in addiction, education, career, or collections. Nothing or no one will fill the place designed in your heart for God alone.

God offers peace and joy.

He gives unconditional love and abundant hope.

Mercy and grace are his trademarks.

His forgiveness is complete and quick and often.

Check out this special invitation from Christ found in Matthew 11:28-30 of *The Message*:

> *"Are you tired? Worn out? Burned out on religion? Come to me. Get away with me and you'll recover your life. I'll show you how to take a real rest. Walk with me and work with me—watch how I do it. Learn the unforced rhythms of grace. I won't lay anything heavy or ill-fitting on you. Keep company with me and you'll learn to live freely and lightly."*

All you have to do is to accept his invitation. Believe in him and trust him. When you accept his offer, he will lead you on a better path for your life than what you could ever manage alone.

And once you partner with him and surrender your future to him, he will be kind and loving and faithful to you. Forever.

You will also have the additional option of allowing him to install an internal GPS system to guide you in the way you should go. He will lay out your steps and coach you all the way through to your finish line with the help of his spirit.

And it's not going to be difficult and uncomfortable. His strand does not include a list of 522 things you are not allowed to do anymore. Rather, God gives us the freedom to make our own choices as we serve him.   And the more we hang with him, the freer and lighter our living (day-by-day details and big picture, future-oriented stuff) becomes.

God wants what's best for you. He is for you, not against you. It took a lot of years of bad religious training before I understood the precious and personal nature of God. He is for us!

Hand him your little wrinkled plastic bag. In his loving kindness, he will pull all those precious loose pearls of your life together in one beautiful strong strand.

And that, my friend, will be a pretty darn classy look on you!

—

If you need someone to explain salvation more clearly, reach out to a local community of believers or connect with me.

If you've been a believer for a while but haven't fully allowed God to pull it all together for you, maybe it's time. Give fully surrendered living a chance for sixty days.   You'll   love   the difference he makes in your life.

Afterword

One day, on a call with a writing coach, I was told people write books in a weekend or two and self-publish without shame. That news shook my world. My previous attempts had taken me years to complete and the manuscripts still remained unpublished in a drawer.

About the same time, the thoughts of this book had been rattling around for a couple of months. Since I love a good challenge, and benefit from a hard deadline (although most often self-imposed), that afternoon after the call, I drafted out a list of eight possible chapters.

Then I wrote. Not in a Word document but on tiny legal pads. And not in my usual obsessive and proper way, but I wrote an imaginary response with an unknown friend after she asked, "Would you tell me how you've made such a great life?"

People do ask me that often.

In 2010, I struggled and wrestled with the supposed American Dream. From all appearances—house, car, career, retirement funds, insurance policies, vacations, discretionary money—I had arrived.

But I was miserable.

In what looked like a completely irrational and scary decision to many, I stepped away from it all so I could pursue a dream that had simmered in me for far too long.

Since then, I've pursued my passion, visited some amazing places, moved cross-country twice, and have accomplished my lifelong desire of living on a beach. I have loads of awesome friends sprinkled in many states, an amazing dream board and a dwindling bucket list.

More incredibly than not, though, I've done this while working insignificant part-time jobs. And my great, big "fabulous" life has been sustained at, or sometimes well below, the national poverty line.

So, yeah, I'm a little non-traditional. (Some people say weird.)

And, sure, I may have overdone Henry David Thoreau's advice to simplify.

I do rely heavily on prayer and my faith, however. You have to when you're this age and have no health coverage.

But, girl, have I created a life I absolutely love!

People say I'm lucky; I like to think blessed, or even favored. With just enough tenacity and crazy to take risks, I hold more optimism than one person should be allowed. I love jumping from small edges. I find great joy in helping others find their thin edge as well.

I have designed the life I wanted and needed in order to feel truly alive, and took notes along the way. Those notes are now my philosophy for living and what I've included here in the principles of this little book. This is the answer to that question I hear so often, "How do you have such an incredible life?"

I hope you hear and appreciate my casual voice and the wisdom God and experience have blessed me with.

And I pray you begin to live with courageous determination from now until your end!

Now, go out there and *Spunkify Your Life*!

About the Author

Cynthia Mendenhall is the Founder and Lead Coach of Spunky Hope, LLC, a company that specializes in helping women redesign their lives, especially after divorce, depression, disease, general despondency, or the death of someone special.

Cynthia is available for personal life coaching, online accountability groups, workshops, seminars, and speaking engagements. You may contact her at www.SpunkyHope.com or like her Spunky Hope Facebook page.

Sign up for her news updates to receive more tips. This will make you one of the first to know about future book releases, online course offerings, retreats, workshops, and scheduled speaking engagements. You may also connect on Twitter, Instagram, and LinkedIn.

And if you make it to the Grand Strand in the near future, look for her poolside, walking the beach, or writing in a local coffee shop.

She'll be the one with the biggest smile.

spunkyHOPE

My Prayer for You

*I pray that God, the source of hope, will fill you completely with joy and peace because you trust in him. Then you will **overflow with confident hope** through the power of the Holy Spirit.*

Romans 15:13 - NLT
(emphasis added)

Acknowledgments

A special thank you to:

Gina Trimarco Cligrow who shoved me toward self-publishing and offered some stiff motivation along the way.

My pastor at Barefoot Church, Clay NeSmith, who never stops teaching about the importance of identifying and walking out your God-given purpose.

The Tuesday Night Gals who trusted me to lead them in Bible-based self-discovery and who have cheered and encouraged me along this path.

Old friends and new who allow me to giggle, make memories with them, and use their stories in my talks and writings.

My family—though we be small, we be mighty. I'll love you all forever! #stucklikeglue

To God, for his patience with my rebellious side and for his love and grace no matter what. He is faithful!

And you, for buying my book, please check out your free thank you video here:

spunkyhope.com/welcomevideo

www.ingramcontent.com/pod-product-compliance
Lightning Source LLC
LaVergne TN
LVHW022324080426
835508LV00041B/2563